# Transformed
## Scriptures to Renew Your Mind
## 30 Day Devotional

Stacie L. Buck

*Stacie L. Buck*

# Transformed
## *Scriptures to Renew Your Mind*
## 30 Day Devotional

## Stacie L. Buck

*Diamond Shapers*

INTERNATIONAL, LLC
*Transforming Minds, Transforming Live*

Transformed: Scriptures to Renew Your Mind
30 Day Devotional

Copyright © 2014 by Stacie L. Buck
Published by Diamond Shapers International, LLC
850 NW Federal Highway, Suite 427
Stuart, FL 34994
www.diamondshapers.com

Cover design by PhotoGraphics USA
www.photographicsusa.com

For bulk sales contact Diamond Shapers International, LLC
Email: info@diamondshapers.com
Phone: (772) 287-8849

Unless otherwise noted, all Scripture quotations are taken from The Amplified ® Bible. Copyright © 1954, 1958, 1962, 1964, 1965, 1987 by The Lockman Foundation. Scripture quotations marked NLT are taken from the New Living Translation Copyright © 1996, 2004, 2007 by Tyndale House Foundation.

ISBN-13: 978-0692209110

ISBN-10: 0692209115

*Stacie L. Buck*

# Introduction

### Romans 12:1-2

*I appeal to you therefore, brethren, and beg of you in view of [all] the mercies of God, to make a decisive dedication of your bodies [presenting all your members and faculties] as a living sacrifice, holy (devoted, consecrated) and well pleasing to God, which is your reasonable (rational, intelligent) service and spiritual worship. ²Do not be conformed to this world (this age), [fashioned after and adapted to its external, superficial customs], but be transformed (changed) by the [entire] renewal of your mind [by its new ideals and its new attitude], so that you may prove [for yourselves] what is the good and acceptable and perfect will of God, even the thing which is good and acceptable and perfect [in His sight for you].*

M ost of us have realized by now, using sheer will power to implement permanent and lasting change in our lives doesn't work. Yes, making a change involves our will, because we must first make a choice to change, but the only way to permanently change our behavior and change our lives is to change the way we think. In fact, Romans 12:2 in the New Living Translation says "...***let God transform you into a new person by changing the way you think...***"

How do we become a new person? We are transformed into a new person when we change the way we think. The main purpose of this devotional is to help you transform your life by changing the way you think – renewing your mind.

Over the years the church has done a poor job of instructing Christians on the importance of renewing their minds. I strongly believe there should be a required course called Christianity 101: Renewing the Mind because the lines are often blurred between believers and non-believers. In many instances, we do not see Christians behaving any differently than non-Christians nor are many walking in victory as the

Word of God promises. The root cause in most instances is an unrenewed mind.

So what exactly does it mean to "renew the mind"? I must admit this phrase left me scratching my head for years. I heard it hundreds of times, but never really understood it. I have heard many preachers and teachers say to their audience "you need to renew your mind with the Word of God", but the messages would always stop there. I think when most of us hear this we think it simply means we need to read our Bible more. While that is a critical element of renewing the mind, in order to grasp this concept fully, we must first understand the desired outcome of this process.

A few years ago I was reading a book by Dr. Bill Winston. In the book, he used a simple illustration about what it means to have a renewed mind. I became so excited because I finally understood what it meant.

Bill Winston compared renewing the mind with learning how to ride a bike. When we get on a bicycle for the first time all of our focus is on riding the bike. When we are on that bike we aren't focused on anything except doing what we need to do to keep from falling over and injuring ourselves. We aren't thinking about anything else in that moment other than what we need to do to keep the bike up and moving, but eventually we learn to ride the bike and it becomes second nature to us. We get to the point where we can ride the bike without even thinking about it. We don't need to go through a mental checklist of how to get on the bike and what we need to do to keep from falling over; we just get on the bike and ride without ever giving a thought to how we are doing it.[1]

After I read this illustration I also thought about how it is similar to learning how to drive a car. At first we may feel overwhelmed with everything involved in driving a car, but eventually we get to the point where even when we are driving we aren't consciously thinking about what we need to do or how we need to do it to get where we want to go.

Have you ever been driving a distance in your car, reached your destination and then realized your mind had been on something else the entire drive? We have all been there! Although our conscious mind may have been preoccupied with our to-do list or an argument we may have had earlier that day, our subconscious mind was able to carry out the function of driving for us.

Both of these activities and many others become second nature to us. We are able to carry them out automatically never thinking about the individual steps involved as we are doing the activity.

So how does this relate to a renewed mind? Just as these activities become second nature to us, certain behaviors and actions should also become second nature to us. We are instructed to renew our mind with the Word of God, God's thoughts and ideas, so His thoughts and words will become second nature to us enabling us to automatically think and act like Him.

What a revelation for me! The goal is to be so full of God's Word no matter where I am, no matter what I am doing, no matter what happens I can automatically act in accordance with God's will and His word without even thinking about how or what to do. It should flow naturally!

When we renew our mind and exchange our thoughts and ideas for God's thoughts and ideas He has provided in His Word we will be TRANSFORMED and walking in the perfect will of God for our lives. It may not happen overnight because renewing the mind is a continual process, but at least I finally have revelation of the ultimate goal and hopefully now you do too!

It is important to remember renewing the mind is not merely a one-time event. It is something we must give our attention to on a regular basis.

In life, what things do we need to renew on a periodic basis? We renew various licenses, magazine subscriptions and anti-virus software subscriptions just to name a few.

- Licenses: What happens when we don't renew a license when it expires? We can't drive our car or we can't practice our profession if it's one that is licensed. Basically we cannot carry out our responsibilities and duties in life and do what we need to do. We are in a holding pattern not able to go anywhere.

- Magazine Subscriptions: What happens when we don't renew a magazine subscription? We stop receiving it and we miss out on the latest news and information.

- Anti-Virus Software: What happens when

we don't renew our anti-virus software? Our computer is susceptible to all kinds of viruses and attacks, infecting it and shutting it down.

These same things happen to us spiritually when we don't renew our minds. Just as not renewing a drivers license stops us from going where we need to go, so does failing to renew our minds. Just as failing to renew a magazine subscription stops us from receiving new information, so does failing to renew our minds. Just as failing to renew our anti-virus software leaves our computer vulnerable and our hard drives corrupted, so failing to renew our minds leaves us defenseless and corrupt in our thinking.

The only difference between renewing these items and renewing our minds is the frequency with which we must do so. Our minds must be renewed on a daily basis if we want to be TRANSFORMED.

So now let's take a closer look at our foundational scripture in Romans 12:2 (AMP):

> *"Do not be conformed to this world (this age), [fashioned after and adapted to its external, superficial customs], but be*

*transformed (changed) by the [entire] renewal of your mind [by its new ideals and its new attitude], so that you may prove [for yourselves] what is the good and acceptable and perfect will of God, even the thing which is good and acceptable and perfect [in His sight for you]."*

## TRANSFORM

The word transformed in this verse comes from the Greek word *metamorphoō* which means to change into another form. Vine's Expository Dictionary offers the following definition: to change into another form, "be transformed", the obligation being to undergo a complete change which, under the power of God, will find expression in character and conduct.[2]

*So how can we tell if someone has a renewed mind?* **Evidence of true transformation will be demonstrated by godly character and conduct.**

## RENEW

The word renew in this verse means to renovate. Vine's Expository Dictionary states "to make new - the adjustment of the moral and spiritual vision and thinking to the mind of God, which is designed to have a transforming effect upon the life." It also goes on to say the action described in Romans 12:2 involves a willing response on the part of the believer.[3] **Renewing the mind is an act of your will. It does not automatically happen.**

The purpose of this devotional is to demonstrate to you the importance of a renewed mind and to help you begin to renovate your thinking. You must demolish all of your old ways of thinking and rebuild a foundation of new ways of thinking that are based on God's ways. You are going to replace your thoughts with God's thoughts.

**Are you ready to transform your mind and transform your life? Let's begin.........**

# Day 1

## Romans 7:15-23

*15For I do not understand my own actions [I am baffled, bewildered]. I do not practice or accomplish what I wish, but I do the very thing that I loathe [which my moral instinct condemns]. 16 Now if I do [habitually] what is contrary to my desire, [that means that] I acknowledge and agree that the Law is good (morally excellent) and that I take sides with it. 17However, it is no longer I who do the deed, but the sin [principle] which is at home in me and has possession of me. 18For I know that nothing good dwells within me, that is, in my flesh. I can will what is right, but I cannot perform it. [I have the intention and urge to do what is right, but no power to carry it out.] 19For I fail to practice the good deeds I desire to do, but the evil deeds that I do not desire to do are what I am [ever] doing. 20Now if I do what I do not desire to do, it is no longer I doing it [it is not myself that acts], but the sin [principle] which dwells within me **[fixed and operating in my soul]**. 21So I find it to* *be a law (rule of action of my being) that when I want to do what is right and good, evil is ever present with me and I am subject to its insistent demands. 22For I endorse and delight in the Law of God in my **inmost self [with my new nature].** 23But I discern in my bodily members [in the sensitive appetites and wills of the flesh] a different law (rule of action) at war against the law of my mind (my reason) and making me a prisoner to the law of sin that dwells in my bodily organs [in the sensitive appetites and wills of the flesh].*

---

I suspect there is not one person who has not had a similar dialogue with himself to the one Paul has with himself in Romans 7. The modern day version might go something like this – *What is wrong with me? Why can't I overcome this issue? Why do I keep making the same poor choices over and over again? I know what God's Word says I should do, but why do I fail when it comes to actually doing it?*

As Christians all too often we know what we are supposed to do, yet we struggle with doing the right thing. Why? Paul's statements in verses 20-22 of Romans 7 in the Amplified Bible, shed some light on this universal struggle. He says that his new nature, his born again spirit, delights in the things of God, yet those desires that are contrary to God's Word reside in his soul.

Our soul – mind, will, and emotions – is in conflict with our regenerated spirit. As Paul says the sin principle is fixed and operating in his soul, but his new nature, his regenerated spirit, his inmost self, delights in the Word of God. The moment we accept Jesus Christ as our Lord and Savior we are engaged in a battle – a battle between our soul and our new spirit man.

Our spirit is born anew at the time of salvation, but our soul is not. In order to win the battle that rages within, we must renew our minds with the Word of God. Although we are justified before God at the time we are saved, we begin the process of sanctification which occurs as we renew our minds and exchange our thoughts for God's thoughts.

Prior to salvation we have spent years developing wrong mindsets and bad habits. Reprogramming our mind to the point it affects our choices and behavior takes time. We reprogram our mind, or renew our mind by studying and meditating on the Word of God.

## Exercise

List those areas in which you are struggling to change your behavior. Identify at least one Scripture for each item and meditate on each daily.

## Prayer

Heavenly Father I realize I cannot be transformed apart from You and the power of Your Word. Help me to overcome those thoughts and desires that dwell within me that are not pleasing to You. Give me the desire to become better acquainted with You and Your ways and give me a greater hunger for Your Word.

# Day 2

## 2 Corinthians 10:3-5

*3For though we walk (live) in the flesh, we are not carrying on our warfare according to the flesh and using mere human weapons. 4For the weapons of our warfare are not physical [weapons of flesh and blood], but they are mighty before God for the overthrow and destruction of strongholds, 5[Inasmuch as we] refute arguments and theories and reasonings and every proud and lofty thing that sets itself up against the [true] knowledge of God; and we lead every thought and purpose away captive into the obedience of Christ (the Messiah, the Anointed One),*

---

The Greek word for stronghold used in this passage is *oxýrōma* which literally means "a heavily fortified containment." A stronghold can be described as a fortress in the mind that protects itself against attack.

Figuratively *oxýrōma* speaks of a false argument in which a person seeks "shelter" to escape reality.[4]

Many of us have strongholds operating in our lives yet we don't even realize it because a stronghold protects itself. When confronted, the stronghold does not allow us to see the truth when it is presented. A stronghold dodges and makes excuses. It creates a false argument in our mind, convincing us what we believe is truth, when in fact what we believe is a lie.

Taking our thoughts captive to the obedience of Christ means we must test our thoughts as to whether or not they line up with the Word of God. If they do not, we need to counter the contradiction to God's Word, by renouncing and refusing to accept the contrary thought. We must then speak out the Word of God concerning that particular subject. For example, when the thought comes to your mind that says you are unworthy of love, you must reject that thought and replace it with the truth of God's Word which says you are worthy and you are loved by God unconditionally. By taking our thoughts captive to the obedience of Christ, strongholds cannot be established.

This is why renewing our mind with the Word of God is critical. How can we know what is contrary to the Word of God, if we do not know what God says? The true knowledge of God has been provided to us in His written Word. It is only in knowing what the Word says that we are able to identify those thoughts that contradict the Word of God. The Word of God is the most powerful weapon of our warfare in tearing down strongholds and preventing them from being established, therefore we must use it daily!

## Exercise

Make a list of the negative thoughts that most commonly run through your mind. Now write out what God would say to you concerning those thoughts. Find a Scripture to support what God would say. Meditate on these Scriptures daily to reinforce what God says.

## Prayer

Father God, I ask for You to reveal to me any strongholds at work in my mind preventing me from receiving Your truth. Holy Spirit, help me to continually identify any thoughts that come into my mind that are contrary to your Word and replace those thoughts with Your thoughts.

# Day 3

## Colossians 3:1-2

*If then you have been raised with Christ [to a new life, thus sharing His resurrection from the dead], aim at and seek the [rich, eternal treasures] that are above, where Christ is, seated at the right hand of God. ²And set your minds and keep them set on what is above (the higher things), not on the things that are on the earth. ³ For [as far as this world is concerned] you have died, and your [new, real] life is hidden with Christ in God.*

———————————

In this passage we are instructed to set our minds on "higher things" meaning we must have a mindset focused on spiritual things. So what exactly is a mindset? To put it simply, a mindset is a habitual way of thinking. We must train ourselves in developing a habit of thinking God's thoughts. When our thoughts are contrary to God's Word, we must learn to exchange our thoughts for God's thoughts.

As Christians, the spiritual realm should be more

real to us than the natural, physical realm. Does this mean we deny the facts or circumstances present in front of us? Absolutely not! It simply means we must recognize God is the highest authority and His will always prevails when we are operating in accordance with His Word, even when circumstances in the natural seem to communicate the contrary. We cannot allow ourselves to be so caught up in our earthly circumstances we become paralyzed in our walk with God. We are in the world, but we are not of the world.[5] We are dead to the world and alive in Him. Our new reality is in Christ. What we see now is only temporary.[6]

Begin to renew your mind, by setting your mind and keeping it set on the Word of God.

## Exercise

Other than those thoughts you identified on Day 2, what other thoughts dominate your mind? Are those thoughts in agreement with God's Word? Search Scripture and find out God's Truth and choose to keep your mind set on what God says.

## Prayer

Thank you, Father God I have been raised to a new life in Christ. Help me to exchange my ungodly thoughts for Your thoughts and help me to keep my mind set on Your Word.

# Day 4

## Colossians 3:9-10

*"...for you have stripped off the old (unregenerate) self with its evil practices, ¹⁰And have clothed yourselves with the new [spiritual self], which is [ever in the process of being] renewed and remolded into [fuller and more perfect knowledge upon] knowledge after the image (the likeness) of Him Who created it."*

---

T he New Living Translation says *"and be renewed as you learn to know your Creator and become like him."* So how do we get to know someone? We spend time with them and we listen to what they have to say to us. We get to know our Creator by setting aside time to spend with Him on a continual basis and by positioning ourselves to hear what He has to say to us. We get to know Him by reading and studying the written, logos Word and listening for His voice, the rhema Word. By getting to know His

Word, we are molded into His image, and we begin to think and act like God.

The only way true transformation can occur is by the knowledge of God through both revelation and application. Most of us have heard "when you know the truth, the truth will set you free," but is that really a true and accurate statement? No. Knowing the truth doesn't set you free, it's applying the truth that sets you free. Often this statement is taken out of context. John 8:31-32 reads:

> *31 So Jesus said to those Jews who had believed in Him, If you abide in My word [hold fast to My teachings and live in accordance with them], you are truly My disciples. 32 And you will know the Truth, and the Truth will set you free.*

First, what is the Truth? Jesus is the Truth. He said in John 14:6 "I am the Way, the Truth and the Life..." When you know Jesus (Truth), Jesus (Truth) will set you free. So how do you get to know the Truth (Jesus)? By abiding in His Word and allowing it to abide in you.

Knowing what the Word says is very different from abiding in the Word and having the Word abide in you. Abide means to accept or act in accordance with something. Head knowledge is useless without application. If the Word abides in you, then you will be living out that knowledge, rather than just mentally acknowledging it.

For the Word to abide in us, we must renew our minds. As we study the Word of God and spend time with Him, we begin to know God more intimately and we become better acquainted with His will and His ways.

## Exercise

In what areas do you know what the Word of God says, but are struggling to believe it and apply it?

## Prayer

Lord give me the desire not just to know Your Word, but to abide in your Word and have Your Word abide in me. My desire is for Your Truth to change me and set me free from the lies embedded in my soul. I know as I commit myself to studying your Word and renewing my mind, Your Truth will transform me from the inside out.

# Day 5

### Hebrews 4:11-12

*11Let us therefore be zealous and exert ourselves and strive diligently to enter that rest [of God, to know and experience it for ourselves], that no one may fall or perish by the same kind of unbelief and disobedience [into which those in the wilderness fell]. 12 For the Word that God speaks is alive and full of power [making it active, operative, energizing, and effective]; it is sharper than any two-edged sword,* **penetrating to the dividing line of the breath of life (soul) and [the immortal] spirit,** *and of joints and marrow [of the deepest parts of our nature], exposing and sifting and analyzing and judging the very thoughts and purposes of the heart.*

---

I n Hebrews 4, we are admonished about suffering the same fate as the Israelites in the wilderness. The Israelites perished without fulfilling God's will for them which was to inherit the Promised Land. God had delivered them from bondage in Egypt, yet they died in the wilderness before reaching their destination.

Unfortunately many Christians today are suffering the same fate. We are delivered at the time of salvation, yet we wander around in the wilderness because of our unbelief. Hebrews 4 tells us how we can avoid the same fate. We must allow the Word of God to examine our innermost thoughts and beliefs.

Notice verse 11 says it was the "unbelief and disobedience" that caused the Israelites to perish, but more specifically, wasn't it their unbelief that caused their disobedience? They praised God for His miracles, but quickly transitioned into grumbling and complaining at any sign of adversity or trouble. If they truly believed what God had promised them, they would have forged forward as He instructed without wavering. They would not have wanted to retreat at the first sign of a challenge. The downfall of the Israelites was that their minds were not renewed to God's ways.

The Greek word for "two-edged" is *dístomos* which when used figuratively means "what penetrates at every point of contact, coming in or going out."[7] When we drink in the Word it penetrates deep within us. When we speak out the Word, it penetrates deep within us and into those around us. We must allow the Word to permeate our soul and root out those areas of unbelief and disobedience. We must feed on it continually until we believe it whole heartedly; not just agreeing with it intellectually, but knowing deep within that it is true and it is true for us.

When we study and meditate on the Word of God our minds become renewed to His ways. How do we know if our thoughts are godly thoughts? We must judge them against the Word of God. Our renewed spirit bears witness with the truth as we read the Word or as God speaks directly to us. The study of God's Word helps our soul – mind, will, and emotions – come into agreement with our regenerated spirit man. The Word examines our innermost thoughts – the unspoken things that often go unnoticed, but the Sword cuts deep to expose those things so we may be transformed.

## Exercise

In Psalm 26:2 Kind David says, *"Examine me, O Lord, and prove me; test my heart and my mind."* Are you willing to ask God to do the same in your life?

## Prayer

Lord, search my heart and my mind and reveal to me anything not pleasing to You. I thank You as I commit to studying Your Word, Your Word will search my heart and I will be transformed by the power of Your Word.

# Day 6

## I Peter 5:8

*8Be well balanced (temperate, sober of mind), be vigilant and cautious at all times; for thatenemy of yours, the devil, roams around like a lion roaring [in fierce hunger], seeking someone to seize upon and devour.*

———————————

W e have an enemy who seeks to destroy us and one of his tactics is to invade our thought life. He seeks to cause chaos and confusion to prevent us from thinking clearly. In a stressful situation what we really believe will manifest itself. It is easy to talk the talk when all is well, but what about when all hell breaks loose? The real you will always come out under pressure.

When someone is intoxicated with alcohol, he or she may say and do things they wouldn't normally say and do – things they often regret afterwards. Does it mean it isn't them doing it? Of course not! Those thoughts and desires were underneath the surface all along, but it was the intoxicated state of the person that caused them to act on them. When we ingest worldly thoughts and ideas instead of godly thoughts and ideas we behave in a manner consistent with what we have been drinking from the world.

We must not allow ourselves to become intoxicated with the things of the world. When we do, we are an easy target for the enemy. We remain vigilant by keeping our minds fixed on God and what He says in His Word. As we submit ourselves to God and resist the devil, he flees from us.[8] He is not able to devour us when we are fully submitted to God. We must submit our soul – mind, will and emotions to God and allow His Word to transform us.

Choose to be sober minded and refuse to drink of the world so you will have the presence of mind to exercise clear judgment in all things.

## Exercise

In what ways are you intoxicated in your thinking? What things are you pursuing? Are your pursuits drawing you closer to God or away from God?

## Prayer

Lord, my desire is to draw closer to you. Give me the desires of Your heart. Thank You I have a sober mind that allows me to hear clearly from You.

# Day 7

## James 1:5-8

*⁵If any of you is deficient in wisdom, let him ask of the giving God [Who gives] to everyone liberally and ungrudgingly, without reproaching or faultfinding, and it will be given him. ⁶Only it must be in faith that he asks with no wavering (no hesitating, no doubting). For the one who wavers (hesitates, doubts) is like the billowing surge out at sea that is blown hither and thither and tossed by the wind. ⁷For truly, let not such a person imagine that he will receive anything [he asks for] from the Lord, ⁸[For being as he is] a man of two minds (hesitating, dubious, irresolute), [he is] unstable and unreliable and uncertain about everything [he thinks, feels, decides].*

---

A superficial reading of this passage of scripture implies God withholds from us when we are double minded, but after closer examination this is not what this scripture means. The Greek word for "receive" used in verse 7 is *lambanó,* which means "to actively lay hold of, to take or receive; to lay hold by aggressively and actively accepting what is offered."[9] Double-mindedness is extremely detrimental to us as it prevents us from taking hold of all that God has already promised to us. A double minded person might be described as a "spiritual schizophrenic" vacillating back and forth between belief and unbelief depending upon his or her circumstances.

So how do we take hold of God's promises? We simply must choose to believe God and to trust in Him and rely on Him. Our unbelief as well as wrong beliefs prevent us from receiving what God has already provided for us. The antidote for doubt and unbelief is faith. To eliminate unbelief, we must renew our minds with the Word of God and receive His truth. As we receive His truth, faith rises up and chokes out the unbelief.

The Israelites were a perfect example of being double minded. They wavered back and forth depending upon their circumstances. True belief stands firm in the face of a challenge. It does not retreat. It does not murmur and complain. It isn't here today and gone tomorrow. Being double minded will keep you stuck. Choose to believe

God, stand firm in that belief so you can lay hold of and accept all that He has already offered to you!

## Exercise

In what areas are you vacillating back and forth between belief and unbelief? Today make a decision to believe what God says about each of those areas.

## Prayer

Lord, forgive me for doubting You and Your Word. Like the man in Mark 9, I ask that You help me overcome my unbelief. Help me to keep my eyes fixed on You and Your Word and not on my circumstances. My desire is to lay hold of all You have to offer me. By faith, I freely receive Your wisdom and guidance.

# Day 8

### Hebrews 12:3

*³Just think of Him Who endured from sinners such grievous opposition and bitter hostility against Himself [reckon up and consider it all in comparison with your trials], so that you may not grow weary or exhausted, losing heart and relaxing and fainting in your minds.*

---

Joyce Meyer wrote a best-selling book *Battlefield of the Mind*. The title speaks for itself. There is a war in our mind and if we faint in our minds we lose the battle.

Our greatest weapon to win the battle, is our mighty Sword - the Word of God. We must read it, speak it and choose to believe it. We gain inner strength by meditating on the Word and renewing our mind with the Word. We begin to faint in our minds when we allow negative thoughts to overtake us, filling us with fear and doubt. Fainting in our minds causes us to give up and resign ourselves to the fact things will not change no matter what we do. A renewed mind does not faint.

In her book Joyce Meyer says "where the mind goes the man follows." We move in the direction of our most dominant thoughts. The state of our mind determines the state of our lives. What we constantly meditate on eventually becomes our reality. If we are defeated in our minds we will live a defeated life. If we are victorious in our minds we will live a victorious life. We must remain vigilant in taking our thoughts captive to the obedience of Christ. Each day we must be determined to win the war in our minds by keeping our minds fixed on the Word of God.

Today make the decision that you will not faint in your mind. Use your mighty Sword to defeat the lies the enemy attempts to plant in your mind.

## Exercise

What is the biggest struggle you are currently facing? Are you expecting victory or defeat? Have you fainted in your mind? If so, find some Scriptures to meditate on and build your faith.

## Prayer

Lord, I thank You Your Word says that I am more than I conqueror. I expect to live the abundant life Jesus died to provide for me. By the power of Your grace, I will not faint in my mind and I will hold fast to the profession of my faith.

# Day 9

## Matthew 4:17

17*From that time Jesus began to preach, crying out, Repent (change your mind for the better, heartily amend your ways, with abhorrence of your past sins), for the kingdom of heaven is at hand.*

---

You might be thinking, *what does a scripture about repentance have to do with renewing the mind?* There is an erroneous belief the word "repent" simply means to ask God for forgiveness; to get before him and say "I am sorry God. Please forgive me." But merely asking for forgiveness is not true repentance. True repentance means to turn and go in another direction and it involves an act of your will and it involves changing your mind. True repentance comes when you choose to adopt a new belief resulting in a changing of your mind to follow the ways of God. The word repent means to change one's mind or purpose – literally to think differently afterwards.[10]

Ask yourself the following questions:

- Is your behavior now any different from your behavior before you were saved?
- Do you think differently than you did before you were saved?

Chances are most people will answer that in some areas their behavior and thinking has changed and in other areas neither has changed. The purpose of asking these questions is not to bring condemnation, but to provide enlightenment regarding those areas in which your mind has not been renewed.

Prior to salvation we have spent years developing wrong mindsets and bad habits. Reprogramming our mind to the point it affects our choices and behavior takes time. We reprogram our mind by studying and meditating on the Word of God.

## Exercise

In what areas are you walking in victory as a result of renewing your mind? In what areas do you need to commit to renewing your mind?

## Prayer

Dear Lord, search my heart and my mind for areas that I have not fully surrendered to You. I am choosing to exchange my thoughts and ways for Your thoughts and ways. Help me to think and act in accordance with Your Word.

# Day 10

## Psalm 139:23-24

*23 Search me [thoroughly], O God, and know my heart! Try me and know my thoughts! 24 And see if there is any wicked or hurtful way in me, and lead me in the way everlasting.*

---

In Psalm 139, David extends an open invitation to God to search His heart for anything that might be unpleasing to Him. Would you be bold enough to pray such a prayer? Too often we get caught up in judging the actions of others that we forget to examine ourselves.

Jeremiah 17:9-10 says:

*9The heart is deceitful above all things, and it is exceedingly perverse and corrupt and severely, mortally sick! Who can know it [perceive, understand be acquainted with his own heart and mind]? 10I the Lord search the mind, I try the heart, even to give to every man*

> *according to his ways, according to the*
> *fruit of his doings.*

Rather than asking God to change our circumstances or change those around us we should ask Him to change us. Like David, we must be bold enough to ask Him to search our hearts and reveal anything that is not pleasing to Him. David was by no means a perfect man, but he sought God continually and he delighted himself in His Word. David may have fallen down at times, but God referred to him as "a man after God's own heart."

It's much easier to place blame outside of ourselves rather than examine ourselves, but we must do so to become all that God has called us to be. A key step in the transformation process is getting honest – honest with yourself and honest with God. You cannot change that which you are unwilling to confront.

## Exercise

Have you been asking God to change your circumstances or perhaps change someone close to you? Is it possible that He could be using those circumstances and relationships to change you?

What changes can you make to improve your relationships and circumstances?

## Prayer

Search me Father God and know my heart. Try me and know my thoughts. Reveal to me if there is any wicked or hurtful way in me. Lead and guide me into Your Truth.

# Day 11

## Ephesians 4:22-24

*22Strip yourselves of your former nature [put off and discard your old unrenewed self] which characterized your previous manner of life and becomes corrupt through lusts and desires that spring from delusion; 23And be constantly renewed in the spirit of your mind [having a fresh mental and spiritual attitude], 24And put on the new nature (the regenerate self) created in God's image, [Godlike] in true righteousness.*

---

How do we strip off our former nature and put on our new nature in Christ? We do so by continually renewing our minds. We must replace our old ways of thinking with godly ways of thinking. As we study and meditate on the Word of God, His truth begins to transform our thinking which in turn changes our behavior.

The Greek word for "renewed" is *ananeóō* which means going up to a higher stage - another level of sanctification - by God's power. It speaks of moving up to new levels of spiritual comprehension and reality. We achieve these new levels as our minds are progressively renewed.[11] Mind renewal is not a one-time event, rather it is a process of learning and accepting truths, one after another. As our minds are renewed we begin to exhibit our new nature in Christ.

The phrase "spirit of your mind", Greek word *nous,* refers to the God given mental capacity of each person to exercise reflective thinking. It is through the spirit of our minds that we receive God's thoughts through faith.[12] Evidence of our transformation occurs as we accept His truth and begin to live in accordance with it.

## Exercise

Verse 24 tells us to put on our new nature created in God's image. Briefly describe the attributes of a person who has adopted the nature of Christ.

## Prayer

Help me Lord to be constantly renewed in the spirit of my mind. Fill me with a deep hunger to study and meditate on Your Word. Thank You for transforming me by the power of Your Word.

# Day 12

## I Corinthians 2:14-16

*14But the natural, nonspiritual man does not accept or welcome or admit into his heart the gifts and teachings and revelations of the Spirit of God, for they are folly (meaningless nonsense) to him; and he is incapable of knowing them [of progressively recognizing, understanding, and becoming better acquainted with them] because they are spiritually discerned and estimated and appreciated. 15But the spiritual man tries all things [he examines, investigates, inquires into, questions, and discerns all things], yet is himself to be put on trial and judged by no one [he can read the meaning of everything, but no one can properly discern or appraise or get an insight into him]. 16For who has known or understood the mind (the counsels and purposes) of the Lord so as to guide and instruct Him and give Him knowledge? **But we have the mind of Christ (the Messiah) and**

### *do hold the thoughts (feelings and purposes) of His heart.*

---

Wow! What a scripture. Did you know as believers we have the mind of Christ? We have the mind of Christ and we hold the thoughts and purposes of His heart.

This truth may be hard to receive because of all of the junk that rolls through our minds on a daily basis. A response to this statement might be *"I have the mind of Christ? Seriously??? I don't think so. Many of the thoughts that go through my mind are far from Christ-like."* This scripture is not referring to our soul possessing the mind of Christ, but rather our regenerated spirit. Prior to salvation we did not have the ability to discern spiritual things, but now that we are saved and have the Holy Spirit living in us we possess the ability to discern spiritual things.

The Greek word *noús* used for mind in verse 16 is the same word used for mind in Ephesians 4:23.[13] It stresses that we possess a God given mental capacity to exercise reflective thinking and receive God's thoughts through faith. We have the capacity to think as Christ thinks as we receive from God through our spirit from the Holy Spirit.

Since we already have the mind of Christ, it is up to us to bring it up from our spirit into our soul – into our mind. We do this by renewing our mind. We come to know His mind by becoming better acquainted with His thoughts and His ways through studying the Word of God. Our renewed spirit bears witness with the truth as we read the Word or as God speaks directly to us. The study of God's Word helps our soul – mind, will, and emotions – come into agreement with our regenerated spirit man.

## Exercise

Verse 16 says we have the mind of Christ. Describe the mind of Christ in your own words.

## Prayer

Lord, I thank You for giving me the mind of Christ. I ask You to help me exchange my thoughts for Your thoughts and allow the mind of Christ to think and operate through my soul so I may demonstrate Your heart and mind to those around me.

# Day 13

## 2 Timothy 1:7

*⁷For God did not give us a spirit of timidity (of cowardice, of craven and cringing and fawning fear), but [He has given us a spirit] of power and of love and of calm and well-balanced mind and discipline and self-control.*

---

If God has given us a spirit of power and of love and a sound mind, why is it that we struggle to operate in this manner? It is because of the battle within our soul due to an unrenewed mind. As the scripture says, we possess all of these characteristics – they are in our regenerated spirit, but our challenge is in getting our soul to line up with our spirit man.

God has not given us a spirit of fear. Fear is an enemy of our soul. When we are filled with fear it is an indicator we do not trust God and we do not believe His Word. Fear is evidence of a mind not yet renewed. A mind renewed by the Word of God, is not influenced by fear. A renewed mind chooses to conduct itself in faith through God's power. We can do anything He requires of us through His power that is at work in us.[14] We simply need to believe and act.

In one of the original Bible translations the phrase "of wise discretion" was used in this passage and in later translations evolved to be interpreted as "sound mind". In the original text, the Greek word *sóphronismos* refers to "acting out God's will by doing what He calls sound reasoning."[15] If God's Word is planted in us, we will have sound reasoning. We will possess the ability to discern and act appropriately in any situation. We gain sound reasoning by renewing our minds. A renewed mind is a sound mind.

## Exercise

In what areas are you struggling with fear? Find Scriptures concerning those areas and meditate on them.

## Prayer

Lord Your Word says You have not given me a spirit of fear, but of power, love and a sound mind. Therefore I choose to walk in Your power and love and with a sound mind. Thank You Lord that as I keep my mind fixed on You and Your Word that fear has no power over me.

# Day 14

### 3 John 1:2

*2Beloved, I pray that you may prosper in every way and [that your body] may keep well, even as [I know] your soul keeps well and prospers.*

------------------------

We are comprised of body, soul and spirit. We are a spirit, our spirit possesses a soul and our spirit lives in a physical body. All three work in tandem with each other. Our soul is the bridge between our spirit and our body and it governs our actions. Therefore, it is our responsibility to get our soul – mind, will and emotions - in alignment with all that God has placed in our regenerated spirit so we will demonstrate right actions. We will not be able to act right, until we believe right. Right believing always precedes right doing. Right believing comes about as we renew our minds with the Word of God.

Since our soul governs our actions, we must first and foremost be well in our soul to live a victorious life. Unfortunately many Christians today suffer from a sick soul. A sick soul not only affects our spiritual walk, but it also affects our physical health. Many scientific studies have proven the adverse effect our thought life has on our physical bodies.

If we are sick in our soul, we will not prosper in life nor prosper in our health as God has planned for us. The word prosper, as it is used in this scripture, refers to being on the right path leading to real success. So what is real success? Real success is fulfilling God's will for our lives. Romans 12:2 tells us to be transformed so we will know the good, acceptable and perfect will of God. Success starts with a renewed mind.

The Greek word used for soul is *psyche* and refers to a person's distinct identity.[16] If we have a false identity due to lies buried deep within our soul we will not prosper. We must learn to identify with Christ and embrace our identity in Him. Your soul prospers when you know who you are in Christ and when you fully embrace and walk in that identity. When your soul prospers, you will prosper in every way!

## Exercise

Are you prospering in your soul? Are you prospering in your body? If not, what changes do you need to make in your life?

## Prayer

Thank you Lord as I study Your Word and submit to You that You are prospering me both soul and body. I will no longer believe the lies of the enemy, but I choose to embrace my identity in Christ. Help me to embrace my identity in You.

# Day 15

## Romans 8:5-7

*⁵ For those who are according to the flesh and are controlled by its unholy desires **set their minds on** and pursue those things which gratify the flesh, but those who are according to the Spirit and are controlled by the desires of the Spirit **set their minds** on and seek those things which gratify the [Holy] Spirit. ⁶ Now the mind of the flesh [which is sense and reason without the Holy Spirit] is death [death that comprises all the miseries arising from sin, both here and hereafter]. But the mind of the [Holy] Spirit is life and [soul] peace [both now and forever]. ⁷ [That is] because the mind of the flesh [with its carnal thoughts and purposes] is hostile to God, for it does not submit itself to God's Law; indeed it cannot.*

---

I n the prior chapter of Romans, Paul described his internal battle, desiring to do what is right, but struggling to do so. As he continues on in Romans 8, he offers some insight on how to overcome the battle.

This passage of Scripture reveals it is our mindset that controls our actions. We must submit our mind to God. Whatever we yield our minds to and submit our minds to will ultimately control our actions. We cannot expect to have godly actions if we do not think godly thoughts.

The Greek word for flesh used here is *sarka* which involves "making decisions according to self; done apart from faith in God." Making decisions according to the flesh, or according to self, results from the untouched parts of us not yet transformed by God.[17] The mind of the flesh is a mindset based solely on sense and reason and operates in contradiction to the Word of God.

Galatians 5:16 instructs us to "walk in the Spirit" and by doing so we will not fulfill the lusts of the flesh. So what does it mean to walk in the Spirit? It means we are living out the Word of God each and every day. And how can we tell if we are walking in the Spirit? If we are walking in the Spirit we will demonstrate the fruit of the Spirit - love, joy, peace, patience, kindness, goodness, faithfulness, gentleness and self control. How do we walk in the Spirit? We can only do so when we renew our minds. The "mind of the spirit" is a mindset that agrees with the thoughts and ways of God.

Our chosen mindset determines the direction of our lives as our inner thoughts determine our outward behavior. Choose wisely!

## Exercise

Are you exhibiting the fruit of the Spirit on a consistent basis? If not, what mindsets might be a hindrance to walking in the Spirit?

## Prayer

Lord my desire is to walk according to the Spirit and for my behavior to demonstrate the fruit of the Spirit. Reveal to me any mindsets that are preventing me from walking in Your will. Help me to keep my mind set on those things that are pleasing to You. Assist me in becoming sensitive to Your leading and not relying on my own sense and reason for making decisions.

# Day 16

## Isaiah 26:3

*³You will guard him and keep him in perfect and constant peace whose mind [both its inclination and its character] is stayed on You, because he commits himself to You, leans on You, and hopes confidently in You.*

---

P eace. We all want it. We yearn for it, yet when we are fortunate enough to find some, it is often short lived as something inevitably comes along to steal it from us. One thing is certain in this life – we are going to face trials and we are going to be challenged. God didn't promise us life would always be easy, but He did promise us He would never leave us nor forsake us.**18** We must come to trust Him in all things and operate in peace regardless of what may come our way.

The NLT Translation says, *"You will keep in perfect peace all who trust in you, all whose thoughts are fixed on you."*

The key to perfect and constant peace is trusting God and keeping our mind focused on Him and His Word in every circumstance of life. When we are confronted with a difficult situation and fearful or negative thoughts begin to bombard our mind, we must reject those thoughts and immediately fix our mind on what the Word of God says concerning our circumstances.

Commit yourself to the Lord. Trust in Him completely. Meditate on His Word continually.

## Exercise

In what areas are you lacking peace? Find at least three Scriptures about the peace of God and meditate on those daily.

## Prayer

Thank you Lord for guarding me and keeping me in perfect peace as my mind is fixed on You and Your Word. I will not be moved by my circumstances. I choose to trust in You because Your Word says You will never leave me nor forsake me.

# Day 17

## Philippians 4:8

*8For the rest, brethren, whatever is true, whatever is worthy of reverence and is honorable and seemly, whatever is just, whatever is pure, whatever is lovely and lovable, whatever is kind and winsome and gracious, if there is any virtue and excellence, if there is anything worthy of praise, think on and weigh and take account of these things [fix your minds on them].*

---

A n important step in renewing our mind involves taking inventory of our thought life. In Philippians, Paul provides us with a checklist for judging our thoughts. He instructs us to think on these things and weigh them – to fix our minds on them.

What does it mean to fix your mind on something? It means you lay hold of it in your mind and firmly hold to it and do not easily let go of it. A fixed mindset is one that is firmly held or fastened in place. Concerning our thoughts, a fixed mindset is an inflexibly held belief. When we have our mind fixed on the Word of God, it means we do not allow our mind to be distracted from godly things.

Use this Scripture as a guide to evaluate your thoughts. If your thoughts are not meeting these criteria, then it is time to do some serious renovation on your mind and renew your thought life.

## Exercise

What are three thoughts you are meditating on most frequently? Use Philippians 4:8 to evaluate those thoughts.

## Prayer

Dear Lord, help me to identify thoughts that are not pleasing to You and help me to take those thoughts captive to the obedience of Christ. Show me the truth of Your Word in each of these areas.

# Day 18

## Hebrews 3:10-12

*10And so I was provoked (displeased and sorely grieved) with that generation, and said, They always err and are led astray in their hearts, and they have not perceived or recognized My ways and become progressively better and more experimentally and intimately acquainted with them. 11 Accordingly, I swore in My wrath and indignation, They shall not enter into My rest. 12[Therefore beware] brethren, take care, lest there be in any one of you a wicked, unbelieving heart [which refuses to cleave to, trust in, and rely on Him], leading you to turn away and desert or stand aloof from the living God.*

---

The story of the Israelites provides us with many valuable lessons, but perhaps one of the most valuable we can glean from their story is the consequences of not trusting God. It was God's will to lead them into the Promised Land and provide them with a life of abundance, yet the generation that came out of Egypt died in the wilderness on the border of the Promised Land.

What kept the Israelites out of the Promised Land? It was their disobedience caused by their unbelief. God told them to go in and possess the land, but rather than obeying His direction, they chose to focus on all of the reasons why they were not able to take the land. Although they witnessed God's miraculous provision for them over and over again, they still did not believe they could go in and possess the land.

The Israelites had a defeated "slave" mentality, seeing themselves as a slave to their circumstances. They couldn't see beyond the obstacles in front of them even though God had already promised them victory. The Israelites were a perfect example of being double minded. They wavered back and forth between belief and unbelief depending upon their circumstances. God's intention was to use the time in the desert to prepare their hearts and minds; to build their trust and confidence in Him so they would take the Promised Land, but their minds had not become renewed during their journey.

We must be diligent in renewing our minds with God's Word, as unbelief causes us to turn away from God and miss the abundant life He has prepared for us. We must progressively become better acquainted with His ways to enter the rest of God. So how do we enter the rest of God? We simply need to believe God's Word and place our complete trust in Him.

Obedience to God hinges upon believing Him. If we believe God and trust Him then we will be obedient to His Word and do as He instructs even in the face of what we may characterize as impossibilities. Unbelief places God at a distance, but belief draws us closer to God.

Draw closer to God today. Simply choose to believe Him!


## Exercise

In what areas are you struggling to believe God? Why are you struggling to believe in each of these areas? Go to the Word of God and find scriptures to encourage yourself in these areas.

## Prayer

Lord, help me to become better acquainted with You and Your ways as I commit to reading Your Word and renewing my mind. As I renew my mind, help me to enter Your rest as I choose to put my trust and confidence in You. By doing so, I position myself to receive all You have promised me.

# Day 19

### Galatians 5:16-17

*16But I say, walk and live [habitually] in the [Holy] Spirit [responsive to and controlled and guided by the Spirit]; then you will certainly not gratify the cravings and desires of the flesh (of human nature without God). 17For the desires of the flesh are opposed to the [Holy] Spirit, and the [desires of the] Spirit are opposed to the flesh (godless human nature); for these are antagonistic to each other [continually withstanding and in conflict with each other], so that you are not free but are prevented from doing what you desire to do.*

---

Most of us have realized by now using sheer will power to implement permanent and lasting change in our lives doesn't work. Will power isn't enough. Yes, making a change involves our will, because we must first make a choice to change, but the only way to permanently change our behavior and change our lives is to change the way we think.

Furthermore we can become so focused on what we shouldn't be doing, we don't spend enough time focused on what we should be doing. It isn't enough to stop wrong behavior, rather we must complete the process by replacing it with right behavior.

Remember Paul's struggle in Romans 8? He had the desire to do what was right, but struggled to do right. This is a battle we all are faced with on a continual basis. How do we win the battle between our soul and our spirit man?

Galatians 5:16 instructs us to "walk in the Spirit" and by doing so we will not fulfill the lusts of the flesh. So what does it mean to walk in the Spirit? It means that we are living out the Word of God each and every day. And how can we tell if we are walking in the Spirit? If we are walking in the Spirit we will demonstrate the fruit of the Spirit - love, joy, peace, patience, kindness, goodness, faithfulness, gentleness and self control. So how do we achieve walking in the Spirit? We must commit to renewing our minds. We must get our thoughts in agreement with God's thoughts. When we reprogram our minds to think as God thinks, we possess the ability to walk in the Spirit on a daily basis.

## Exercise

Are you struggling because you are too focused on what you should not be doing rather than focusing on what you should be doing? It isn't enough to make a decision to break a bad habit. Bad habits must be replaced with good ones for true transformation to occur. What habits do you need to break? What habits do you need to adopt to replace those negative habits?

## Prayer

Lord I desire to be guided by Your Holy Spirit each day and to live a life that is pleasing to You. Help me to develop godly habits by the power of Your Spirit working in me.

# Day 20

## Joshua 1:8

*⁸ This Book of the Law shall not depart out of your mouth, but you shall meditate on it day and night, that you may observe and do according to all that is written in it. For then you shall make your way prosperous, and then you shall deal wisely and have good success.*

---

Although we are living in the dispensation of grace and we are no longer living under the law, the same principle of meditating on God's Word still holds true for Christians today. We can't live in accordance with God's Word unless we know what it says and take the time to become intimately familiar with it. To meditate means to murmur or to ponder.[19] Meditating involves not only thinking on God's Word, but speaking God's Word as well.

How do you commit something to memory? You say it over and over again. Eventually you don't even need to think about the words, they just flow out naturally. When we are in the process of renewing our minds our goal should be the same - to become so full of God's Word that we are speaking it out and acting on it without having to think about it. It should just naturally flow through our words and our behavior.

God's Word is full of wisdom that will lead us to success when we give attention to it and apply it on a daily basis.

## Exercise

How often do you read the Word of God? How much time do you spend meditating on the Word of God? Commit to meditating on at least one Scripture per day that will encourage you and build your faith.

## Prayer

I thank you Lord that You have given me an instruction manual for living a successful life. I ask that You place within me a burning desire to feed on Your Word each and every day and to meditate on it day and night. My desire is to become so consumed by Your Word that I am not moved by the storms of life. Thank you for providing me with Your knowledge and wisdom.

# Day 21

## Proverbs 2:1-5

*My son, if you will receive my words and treasure up my commandments within you, [2]Making your ear attentive to skillful and godly [a]Wisdom and inclining and directing your heart and mind to understanding [applying all your powers to the quest for it]; [3]Yes, if you cry out for insight and raise your voice for understanding, [4]If you seek [Wisdom] as for silver and search for skillful and godly Wisdom as for hidden treasures, [5]Then you will understand the reverent and worshipful fear of the Lord and find the knowledge of [our omniscient] God.*

---

If someone provided you with a treasure map and guaranteed you success in finding the buried treasure by following the map, would you set out to find the treasure? Of course you would! Think of all of the wonderful things you could do with your new found riches. We should search the Word of God with as much determination and excitement as we would a lost treasure.

The Bible is a priceless treasure chest filled with nuggets more precious than silver or gold yet too often we neglect reading and studying it. To know God's Word is to know the heart of God towards us. His Word not only proclaims His never ending unconditional love for us, but He has given us every instruction we need for living a prosperous life.

We should seek to possess God's knowledge and wisdom with the same zeal we would a lost treasure. We must cry out to God for a deeper understanding of His Word and ask for His grace in applying His principles.

Rather than seeking more things, we must seek more of God. When we seek Him first then all that we need will be supplied for us.[20] The most valuable currency we can possess is the Word of God. The best part about God's currency is as we spend it by speaking it, our supply can be replenished each day.

## Exercise

What things are you pursuing on a daily basis? How much time do you spend pursuing the things of God?

## Prayer

Thank you, Lord for the endless supply of Your Word which is more precious than silver and gold. I choose to search for the hidden treasures You have for me rather than pursuing the pleasures of this world. I know that as I pursue You, You will supply everything I need.

# Day 22

## Psalm 1:1-3

*Blessed (happy, fortunate, prosperous, and enviable) is the man who walks and lives not in the counsel of the ungodly [following their advice, their plans and purposes], nor stands [submissive and inactive] in the path where sinners walk, nor sits down [to relax and rest] where the scornful [and the mockers] gather.* *2 But his delight and desire are in the law of the Lord, and on His law (the precepts, the instructions, the teachings of God)* **he habitually meditates (ponders and studies) by day and by night. 3And he shall be like a tree firmly planted [and tended] by the streams of water, ready to bring forth its fruit in its season; its leaf also shall not fade or wither; and everything he does shall prosper [and come to maturity].**

Trees get nourishment and drink in water from the roots. As long as there is a continual supply of nutrients and water, a tree will flourish. The same is true of our soul. When we are rooted in God and we drink in the water of His Word each day we will bring forth fruit and prosper in all that God has purposed for us to do.

Renewing our minds is not a one-time event. It involves dedicating ourselves to the study of God's Word and meditating on it habitually. We must practice it daily so we will be ready to bring forth fruit when it is the appointed season. The Word sustains us and waters our soul.

When we delight ourselves in the Lord, He will give us the desires of our heart. As we draw close to Him, His desires become our desires. Everything we do will prosper because it is done in accordance with the Word of God.

## Exercise

Do you feel like you have faded or withered in some aspects of your life? Specifically, in which ones? Find three Scriptures to encourage you in those areas and meditate on them daily.

## Prayer

I desire to be like a tree firmly planted by the streams of water bringing forth fruit in its season. I know as I drink nourishment from Your Word and develop a habit of mediating on Your Word, my works will prosper.

# Day 23

## John 15:7

*7If you live in Me [abide vitally united to Me] and My words remain in you and continue to live in your hearts, ask whatever you will, and it shall be done for you.*

---

As Christians we are taught to bring our requests before God in prayer and that He is a God who answers our prayers. But will God really give us anything that we ask for? Does he always answer our prayers? While God does grant many of our requests, some He does not. There are many reasons as to why He may not give us what we are asking for, but one of the reasons is that we are not asking according to His Word.

A key to receiving what we ask God for is asking in accordance with His will which is found in His written Word. So how do we know His will? Our foundational Scripture in Romans 12:2 provides us with the answer:

> ......*but be transformed (changed) by the*
> *[entire] renewal of your mind [by its new*
> *ideals and its new attitude], so that you*
> *may prove [for yourselves] what is the*
> *good and acceptable and perfect will of*
> *God, even the thing which is good and*
> *acceptable and perfect [in His sight for*
> *you].*

As we study the Word of God and spend time with Him, we begin to know God more intimately and we become better acquainted with His will and His ways. He changes us from the inside out and His desires become our desires. When we fill ourselves with His Word, His Words become our words and God's Word does not return void.[21]

## Exercise

Do you have a prayer request that has not yet been answered? If so, go to the Word of God and find a Scripture that supports your request and meditate on it daily.

## Prayer

Go before God and pray the Scripture you identified for your prayer request in the exercise above.

# Day 24

## Isaiah 55:8-9

*8For My thoughts are not your thoughts, neither are your ways My ways, says the Lord. 9For as the heavens are higher than earth, so are My ways higher than your ways and My thoughts than your thoughts.*

———————————

One reason God's thoughts and ways are higher than our thoughts and ways is that He is an omniscient God. He knows everything. He sees our beginning and our end on this earth.

Although we will never know everything there is to know about God's ways, thankfully God has provided us with much of what we need to know in His Word and we can rely on the Holy Spirit to bring clarity to the written Word.

The best way to get to know God's thoughts and ways is by studying the Bible daily to renew our minds with His Word. Renewing the mind is simply exchanging your thoughts for God's thoughts. As our foundational scripture, Romans 12:2 tells us, we are transformed into a new person by the renewing of our mind. When we change the way we think, we are changed. We are not to adapt to the customs of this world we live in, but rather we should be a catalyst for the world to be transformed by the power of God.

### Exercise

Continue reading Isaiah 55 in your Bible, focusing on verse 11. What does this verse mean to you?

### Prayer

Lord as I read and study Your Word, help me to understand Your thoughts and Your ways. Help me to think as You think and act in accordance with Your will for my life.

# Day 25

## Proverbs 16:1-3

*The plans of the mind and orderly thinking belong to man, but from the Lord comes the [wise] answer of the tongue. ²All the ways of a man are pure in his own eyes, but the Lord weighs the spirits (the thoughts and intents of the heart). ³Roll your works upon the Lord [commit and trust them wholly to Him; He will cause your thoughts to become agreeable to His will, and] so shall your plans be established and succeed.*

————————————

There is an old saying "the best-laid plans of mice and men often go awry." Have you ever experienced your plans going awry? You thought you had developed a fool proof plan, but then down the road you found yourself facing a huge mess wishing you had made different choices? Many times experience is the best teacher, but what if there was a way we could shorten the path to success and save ourselves some headaches along the way? The exciting news is there is a way!

As we begin to renew our minds with the Word of God and exchange our thoughts for His thoughts, we become more intimately familiar with His will and His ways. When our thoughts come into agreement with His thoughts, we are able to make our plans in accordance with His will and we will be successful in achieving the desired outcome – His outcome. When our thoughts agree with God's thoughts, our plans will succeed because they are God's plans and not merely our own plans. God knows what we do not as He sees the future when we cannot.

Additionally, we must always check our motives. It is possible to do a right thing for a wrong reason. God examines the hidden motives of our heart and when our motives are pure, God will cause our plans to succeed.

### Exercise

Have you ever experienced your plans going awry? Could the undesirable outcome have been avoided by consulting with God and seeking His wisdom concerning your plans?

## Prayer

Lord, forgive me for thinking my ways are better than Your ways. From now on, I will seek You and Your plan for my life. I know that as I commit my ways and plans to You Lord, You will cause them to ultimately succeed.

# Day 26

## Mark 4:3-8

*3Give attention to this! Behold, a sower went out to sow. 4And as he was sowing, some seed fell along the path, and the birds came and ate it up.5Other seed [of the same kind] fell on ground full of rocks, where it had not much soil; and at once it sprang up, because it had no depth of soil; 6And when the sun came up, it was scorched, and because it had not taken root, it withered away. 7Other seed [of the same kind] fell among thorn plants, and the thistles grew and pressed together and utterly choked and suffocated it, and it yielded no grain. 8And other seed [of the same kind] fell into good (well-adapted) soil and brought forth grain, growing up and increasing, and yielded up to thirty times as much, and sixty times as much, and even a hundred times as much as had been sown.*

---

I n verses 14-20 of Mark 4, Jesus explains the seed in this parable represents the Word of God. Are you experiencing a thirty, sixty or hundred fold return on the Word of God in your life?

For a seed to produce it must be planted in fertile soil. It won't produce a harvest just anywhere. In this parable, the problem wasn't with the seed, the seed was of the same kind. The problem was the ground on which it fell. The Word of God is incorruptible seed that always produces what is intended.[22] If we are not reaping a harvest, we must evaluate the "garden" of our heart.

The seed that fell along the path did not produce any harvest. The birds came and ate the seed. Too often we hear the Word, but it doesn't get planted in our heart. We may mentally agree with it, yet not believe it in our heart. The enemy of our soul convinces us God's Word may work for others, but it will not work for us. He successfully steals the Word from us.

The seed that fell on the stony ground represents us hearing the Word and receiving it with excitement, but because it is not rooted deeply enough, we give up and fall away in the face of any trials and troubles that arise.

The seed that fell among thorns, had enough soil to produce a harvest, but the thorns and thistles prevented a full harvest. Our unresolved soul battles too often crowd out the Word and we do not see the desired fruit.

So how do we receive a harvest of thirty, sixty, or hundred fold on the Word of God? We must identify and remove old ways of thinking and being and replace them with God's Word.

Furthermore, just as a farmer cannot plant seed only one time and expect to reap a continual harvest, we cannot expect to do so without continually renewing our minds.

## Exercise

In what areas of your life are you not reaping your desired harvest? Do you believe what the Word of God says concerning those things? Choose to renew your mind with God's Word concerning these areas.

## Prayer

Lord I thank You for Your Word that is incorruptible seed that always produces its intended harvest. Help me to properly cultivate the garden of my heart so Your Word may be deeply planted and rooted within me producing an abundant harvest in my life.

# Day 27

### Matthew 15:11

*11 It is not what goes into the mouth of a man that makes him unclean and defiled, but what comes out of the mouth; this makes a man unclean and defiles [him].*

### Matthew 12:34-35

*34 ...For out of the fullness (the overflow, the superabundance) of the heart the mouth speaks. 35 The good man from his inner good treasure flings forth good things, and the evil man out of his inner evil storehouse flings forth evil things.*

---

These days there is a significant push to become more health conscious and people are exercising more caution concerning what they are putting in their mouths. Why are so many of us willing to change our eating habits? We do so because we realize the benefits to our general health as well as on the scale. We know we can't eat junk food everyday and expect to maintain our ideal weight and remain healthy. Why are we not as careful about what we feed our mind through our eyes and our ears? When we get hungry we don't go to the nearest trash can or dumpster to find our next meal, so why do we allow garbage to be consumed by our minds?

We have all heard the phrase "garbage in, garbage out." While intended to describe a concept in computer programming, it also can be used to describe what happens when we are giving our attention to the wrong things. Just as a computer can only do what it is programmed to do, we can only do what our minds have been programmed to do. To change our behavior we must change our internal programming. We speak and act from the programs running on the inside of us which are a result of what we have allowed into our mind through our eyes and ears.

When computer programs do not behave as intended by the program designer, the programmer performs a function called "debugging" which is a process of finding and fixing the defects in a computer program so that its functioning will result in the intended outcome. We must make a commitment to submit our minds to the debugging process. We must identify those internal programs that are in conflict with the Word of God and we must remove those programs and replace them with godly programs by renewing our minds.

## Exercise

Do the words you speak give life or bring death? What are you feeding on that is adversely affecting your thoughts and words?

## Prayer

Dear Lord, help me to become more aware of what comes out of my mouth and more aware of what I am allowing into my eyes and ears. Continue to help me identify any hidden beliefs that are preventing me from receiving all that You have for me.

# Day 28

## Proverbs 23:6-7

*⁶ Eat not the bread of him who has a hard, grudging, and envious eye, neither desire his dainty foods; ⁷ For as he thinks in his heart, so is he. As one who reckons, he says to you, eat and drink, yet his heart is not with you [but is grudging the cost].*

---

What is the difference between thinking in your heart and thinking in your mind? We have both a conscious and subconscious mind. The heart can be described as the subconscious mind which houses our internal programs that determine our core beliefs. Our subconscious mind determines our automatic behaviors, but our conscious mind possesses the ability to override those programs when we deem it necessary in certain situations.

In some situations we choose to wear masks by adapting our words and behavior to what we think others expect from us. What one says to others might not actually be what one believes. For example, many people who appear to be arrogant and boastful by their choice of words actually are fearful and insecure. They are afraid for others to know the truth about them, so they put on a mask to make themselves appear overly confident.

Many times we often try to deny what is in our heart, yet we cannot escape it. Even if we manage to fool others, on the inside we are in constant turmoil. Studying the Word of God brings light to those dark areas concealed from sight. Renewing the mind involves getting the Word of God from your head into your heart. Once it is planted and rooted deep in your heart it will be evident in your character and conduct. You will no longer need to pretend to be something you are not, because you will be transformed into the image of Christ.

## Exercise

In what relationships or circumstances do you find yourself regularly wearing a mask? What would happen if you surrendered these areas to God?

## Prayer

Lord, reveal to me any masks I am wearing of which I am not aware. Help me to take off those masks once and for all and put on my identity in Christ.

# Day 29

## Proverbs 17:22

*²²A happy heart is good medicine and a cheerful mind works healing, but a broken spirit dries up the bones.*

## Proverbs 14:30

*³⁰A calm and undisturbed mind and heart are the life and health of the body, but envy, jealousy, and wrath are like rottenness of the bones.*

———————————

What modern science has revealed to us about the mind-body connection, Scripture revealed to us thousands of years ago. Our thoughts not only determine our actions, but our thoughts also affect our health. Your body responds to the way you think and feel. Negative thoughts cause negative emotions and those negative emotions place the body in a state of distress and various health problems begin to manifest. Negative emotions are toxic.

It is believed 80% of all disease is stress related. Prolonged states of stress have been linked to the onset of auto-immune diseases. The word disease literally means "not at ease." When we are living in a constant state of turmoil our mind and body are not at ease. A sick soul can eventually produce a sick body.

The Word of God is life to us – both spiritual and physical. As it nourishes our soul it gives strength and health to our physical body. 3 John 2 tells us our physical body is healthy to the degree our soul prospers and Proverbs 4:20-22 says:

> [20] *My son, attend to my words; consent and submit to my sayings.* [21] *Let them not depart from your sight; keep them in the center of your heart.* [22] *For they are life to those who find them, healing and health to all their flesh.*

The key to emotional and physical well being lay in studying and meditating on the Word of God daily. When we submit ourselves to God and we begin to get our thoughts in agreement with God's Word and we believe His Word and rely on Him and trust Him fully, we no longer will be living in a state of distress. Meditating on His Word brings healing and health to both body and soul.

## Exercise

What situations are currently causing you stress? What steps can you take to alleviate stress in your life?

## Prayer

I thank You Lord as I attend to Your Word it brings health and healing to my soul and body. Help me to maintain a calm and undisturbed mind regardless of the circumstances that surround me.

# Day 30

## 2 Corinthians 4:16

*16Therefore we do not become discouraged (utterly spiritless, exhausted, and wearied out through fear). Though our outer man is [progressively] decaying and wasting away, yet our inner self is being [progressively] renewed day after day.*

---

We can be encouraged regardless of what we may be facing, our situation is only temporary. Although we may be dying on the outside, we are gaining life on the inside. Our inner self is being renewed not just for now but for eternal purposes.

Our spirit is born anew at salvation, but our soul is not. Although we are saved and justified before God, we are not yet sanctified. At the time of salvation we begin the process of sanctification which is achieved by renewing the mind. God rescues us from the bondage and consequences of sin, but He will not renew our minds for us. We must get our soul – our mind, our will and our emotions – to line up with the Word of God to be Spirit led.

## Exercise

When going through difficult circumstances it is important to recall past victories. In your past, which adverse circumstances have transformed you for the better?

## Prayer

Dear Lord no matter what comes my way I will not be discouraged. I know You are for me and You have plans to prosper me and I will have victory. Things may not always come the way I would like, but I know You will provide for me. Thank You for Your grace and mercy You extend to me each and every day as I walk in the process of sanctification and seek to be transformed into all You have called me to be.

# Notes

1. Dr. Bill Winston, *Transform Your Thinking, Transform Your Life,* (Tulsa, OK: Harrison House, 2008)
2. W.E. Vine, *Vine's Concise Dictionary of the Bible* *(Nashville, TN:* Thomas Nelson, 2005)
3. Ibid.
4. http://biblehub.com/greek/3794.htm
5. John 15:19
6. 2 Corinthians 4:18
7. http://biblehub.com/greek/1366.htm
8. James 4:7
9. http://biblehub.com/greek/2983.htm
10. http://biblehub.com/greek/3340.htm
11. http://biblehub.com/greek/365.htm
12. http://biblehub.com/greek/3563.htm
13. Ibid.
14. Ephesians 3:20
15. http://biblehub.com/greek/4995.htm
16. http://biblehub.com/greek/5590.htm
17. http://biblehub.com/greek/4561.htm
18. Hebrews 13:5
19. http://biblehub.com/hebrew/1897.htm
20. Matthew 6:33
21. Isaiah 55:11
22. I Peter 1:23

# About the Author

Stacie L. Buck is the President & Founder of Diamond Shapers International, LLC in Stuart, FL. She is a public speaker, author and life coach. Diamond Shapers International was birthed out of her desire and passion to help others achieve their goals and dreams and fulfill their God given destiny.

After a highly successful career in the healthcare industry Stacie was ready for a new challenge and decided to expand her horizons and take her passion for teaching and employ it on a larger scale to empower individuals to achieve their dreams and goals by overcoming obstacles to success.

Stacie is a gifted speaker and teacher who now uses her own journey of healing and self discovery as a teaching tool for others and she shares insights she has learned from several years of personal study. Stacie's speaking and teaching style is down to earth and she is known for her transparency.

To learn more about Stacie and her speaking, writing and personal coaching services, visit her on the web at www.diamondshapers.com

Follow Stacie on Facebook:
https://www.facebook.com/diamondstacie

Follow Stacie on Twitter: @DiamondStacie

Email Stacie at: info@diamondshapers.com

# Other Books by the Author

## *All Access:  Unlocking the Power of God's Word*

In All Access: Unlocking the Power of God's Word, author Stacie Buck takes you on a journey of self-discovery packed with life changing revelation that will help you achieve freedom in every area of your life.

Specifically Stacie leads you in how to:

- Clear your path of all the obstacles holding you back from living the victorious and abundant life you have been missing out on;

- Renew your mind and change the way you think about God, yourself and others;

- Recognize negative patterns in your life and understand how they reveal your inner beliefs;

- Embrace your true identity in Christ;

- Win the battles raging in your soul and overcome shame , fear, rejection and more!

Order *All Access: Unlocking the Power of God's Word*, at http://www.diamondshapers.com/product-category/products/

# Need a Speaker for your small group or next event?

*Stacie shows you how to transform your life by transforming your mind.*

## Stacie will lead you in how to:

- Renew your mind and change the way you think about God, yourself and others.

- Recognize negative patterns in your life and understand how they reveal your inner beliefs.

- Identify hindrances that are keeping you from God's best for you.

- Clear your path of all the obstacles holding you back from the victorious and abundant life you have been missing out on.

- Embrace your true identity in Christ.

- Win the "battles" raging in your soul and overcome shame, fear, rejection and more—once and for all!

## What audiences have to say:

*"I have to say that your presentation had to be one of the very best as far as maintaining everyone's interest, your ability to deliver in an effortless way*

*and interweaving your personal experiences brilliantly. Not only were you clearly knowledgeable about your subject matter, you shared personal experiences with such style, grace and conviction that it touched my heart. I've since been able to use the concepts you shared in both my personal and professional life with true benefits realized."* **~Sue R.**

*"Not only did I enjoy your style of teaching, but you opened yourself up and shared your own struggles for the benefit of others. The more I apply your techniques to my life, the more free I become from all that has held me back for years. Thank you so much for being open to what God wanted you to do, as I believe this is your true calling!"* **~Danielle L.**

*"Stacie has tremendous knowledge and revelation in the area of transforming the mind. She is articulate and well-spoken and uses real life examples to help audience members identify and overcome mindsets that are hindering them from having the lives they desire."* **~Sue L.**

*"Stacie is very inspirational and knowledgeable, and speaks with a comfortable, personable style. She relates to her audience by sharing her own personal experiences and bringing hope to hearts that feel discouraged and hopeless. She is gifted*

*in helping people to shed light onto their path and see the things that are holding them back. Stacie walks them through their metamorphic process, ultimately leading them to wholeness and beauty within, preparing and guiding them to achieve their divine destiny."* **~Deborah B.**

*"Thank you for a wonderful and lively presentation! I appreciate the revelations you made—a difficult illness and your internal struggle with personal demons. Exposing yourself in front of a large group of people, well, I see it as an act of bravery."* **~Craig B.**

*"I always make it a point to attend Stacie's sessions, even when the program has several other options. Her energetic and thought-provoking presentations always provide me with a smile from the insights. It is clear when attending that she has given her heart and soul to presentation preparation in concept, content and delivery. Stacie's genuine presentations will cause you to reflect on your beliefs and be inspired by new concepts."* **~ Perry E.**

Visit http://www.diamondshapers.com/speaking to fill out the speaking request form to schedule Stacie to speak at your next event.

# Contact the Author

Stacie L. Buck

President & Founder

Diamond Shapers International, LLC

850 NW Federal Highway, #427

Stuart, FL 34994

(772) 287-8849

Email: info@diamondshapers.com

www.diamondshapers.com

## Diamond Shapers

# INTERNATIONAL, LLC
*Transforming Minds, Transforming Lives*

### Our Mission
To transform the world by transforming minds and transforming lives.

### Our Vision
To create a world in which those in the body of Christ are operating in their full potential both personally and professionally having maximum impact on the world.

### Our Strategy
To provide education and resources that empower believers to renew their minds, receive God's promises and operate according to His Word.

www.diamondshapers.com

*Diamond Shapers*

# INTERNATIONAL, LLC
*Transforming Minds, Transforming Lives*

## About Diamond Shapers International, LLC

Diamond Shapers International, LLC was founded by Stacie L. Buck. Diamond Shapers International was birthed out of her desire and passion to help others achieve their goals and dreams and fulfill their God given destiny.

Since Stacie was a little girl she has had a passion for teaching and it was a long standing dream of hers to become a teacher. Her path to teaching has certainly been one that is non-traditional. She graduated Magna Cum Laude with a Bachelor of Science Degree from Health Information Management and spent twenty two years working in the healthcare industry. During her career in health information management she served in many roles, but regardless of her job title her passion still remained – teaching others which fueled her desire to begin her own consulting business. For over a dozen years Stacie provided education to those within her organization as well as to outside organizations. She is a nationally known speaker and author for her healthcare specialty and she has taught several courses at the local state college.

In addition to her love for teaching, Stacie enjoys serving others and mentoring others. During her healthcare career she served in numerous volunteer positions and leadership roles and received numerous service awards, including the Mentor Award from the American Health Information Management Association. Her peers describe her as a leader who inspires others and elevates the performance of those around her. Stacie is also known for taking complex subject matter and making it simple for her students.

After a highly successful career in the healthcare industry Stacie was ready for a new challenge and decided to expand her horizons and take her passion for teaching and employ it on a larger scale to empower individuals to achieve their dreams and goals by overcoming obstacles to success.

www.diamondshapers.com